Martin LUTHER KING, Jr.

Lily Erlic

Lightbox is an all-inclusive digital solution for the teaching and learning of curriculum topics in an original, groundbreaking way. Lightbox is based on National Curriculum Standards.

OPTIMIZED FOR

- ✓ **TABLETS**
- ✓ **WHITEBOARDS**
- ✓ **COMPUTERS**
- ✓ **AND MUCH MORE!**

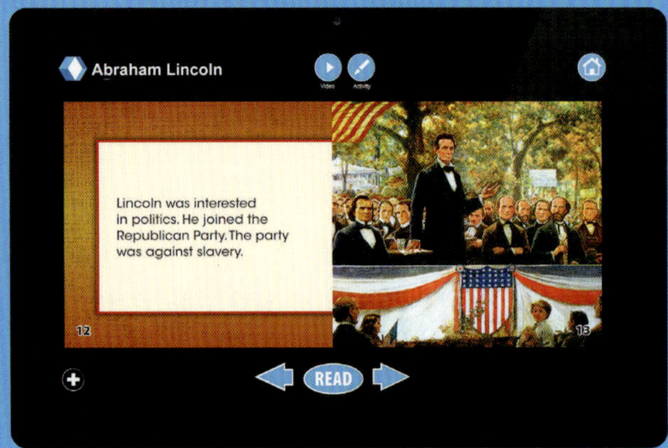

STANDARD FEATURES OF LIGHTBOX

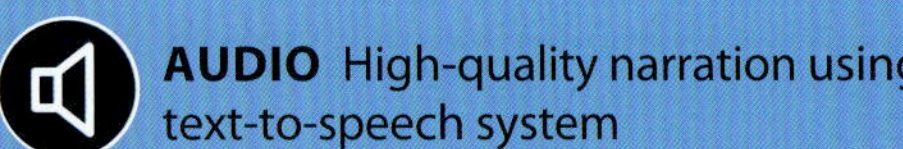
AUDIO High-quality narration using text-to-speech system

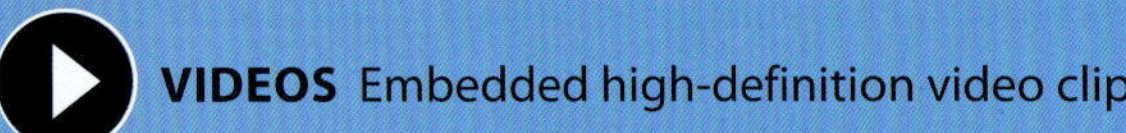
VIDEOS Embedded high-definition video clips

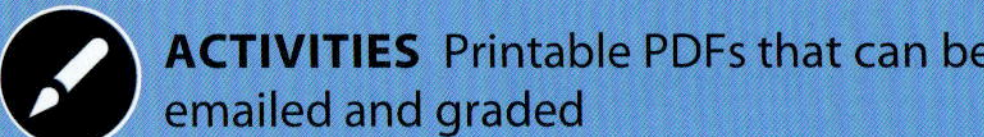
ACTIVITIES Printable PDFs that can be emailed and graded

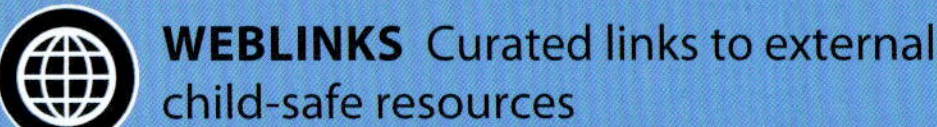
WEBLINKS Curated links to external, child-safe resources

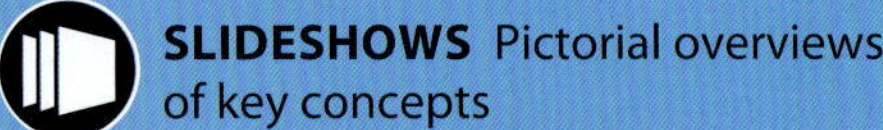
SLIDESHOWS Pictorial overviews of key concepts

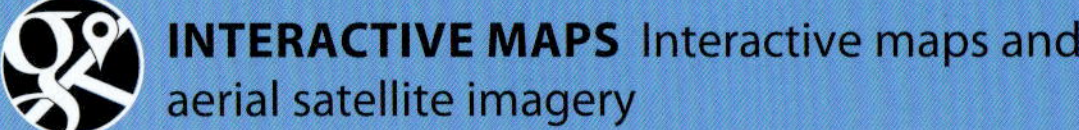
INTERACTIVE MAPS Interactive maps and aerial satellite imagery

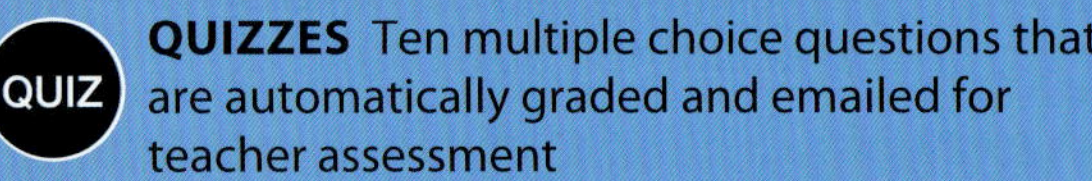
QUIZZES Ten multiple choice questions that are automatically graded and emailed for teacher assessment

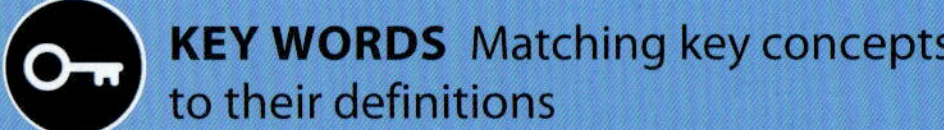
KEY WORDS Matching key concepts to their definitions

VIDEOS

WEBLINKS

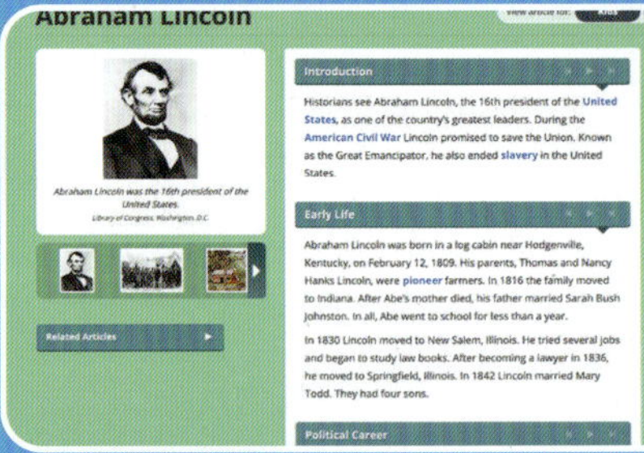

SLIDESHOWS

QUIZZES

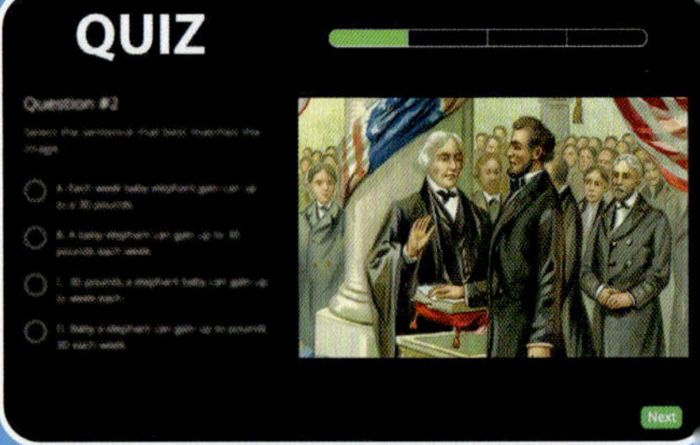

Martin LUTHER KING, Jr.

Contents

Martin Luther King, Jr. was one of the most important civil rights leaders in U.S. history.

King led **25,000** people in a march to promote **equality**.

King was born in Georgia. He lived in his grandparents' house.

More than 100 streets in Georgia are named after King.

Some people did not like African Americans. King and other African Americans were sometimes treated poorly.

Cafeteria
PARKING IN REAR
EXIT ONLY

King became a Baptist minister. He preached that all people should be treated equally.

Civil rights are rights given by the government of a place to the people living there.

African Americans did not have many civil rights. King worked to change that.

TELEPHONE
CANADA TOO

King believed that people should not be treated differently just because of the color of their skin.

"The time is always right to do what is right."
- Martin Luther King, Jr.

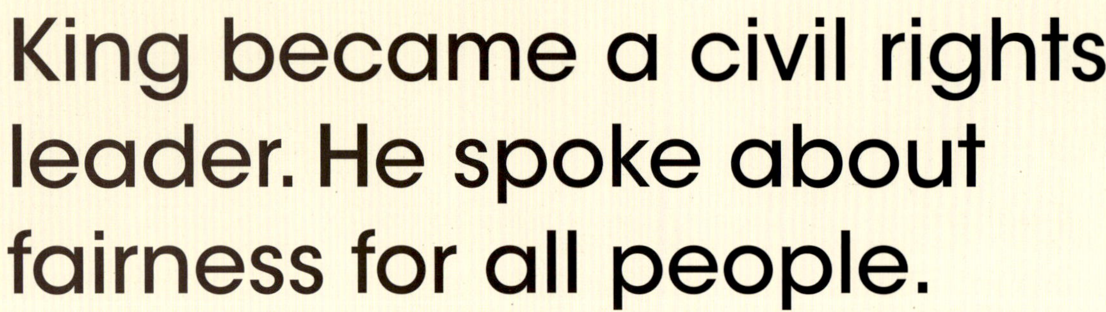

King became a civil rights leader. He spoke about fairness for all people.

King gave speeches more than **2,500 times**.

MARCH ON WASHINGTON
JOBS & FREEDOM

King's most famous speech is called "I Have a Dream." It continues to inspire people today.

King won the Nobel Peace Prize for his work.

More than 3 million people visit the **Martin Luther King, Jr. Memorial** in **Washington, D.C.,** every year.

Martin Luther King, Jr. Timeline

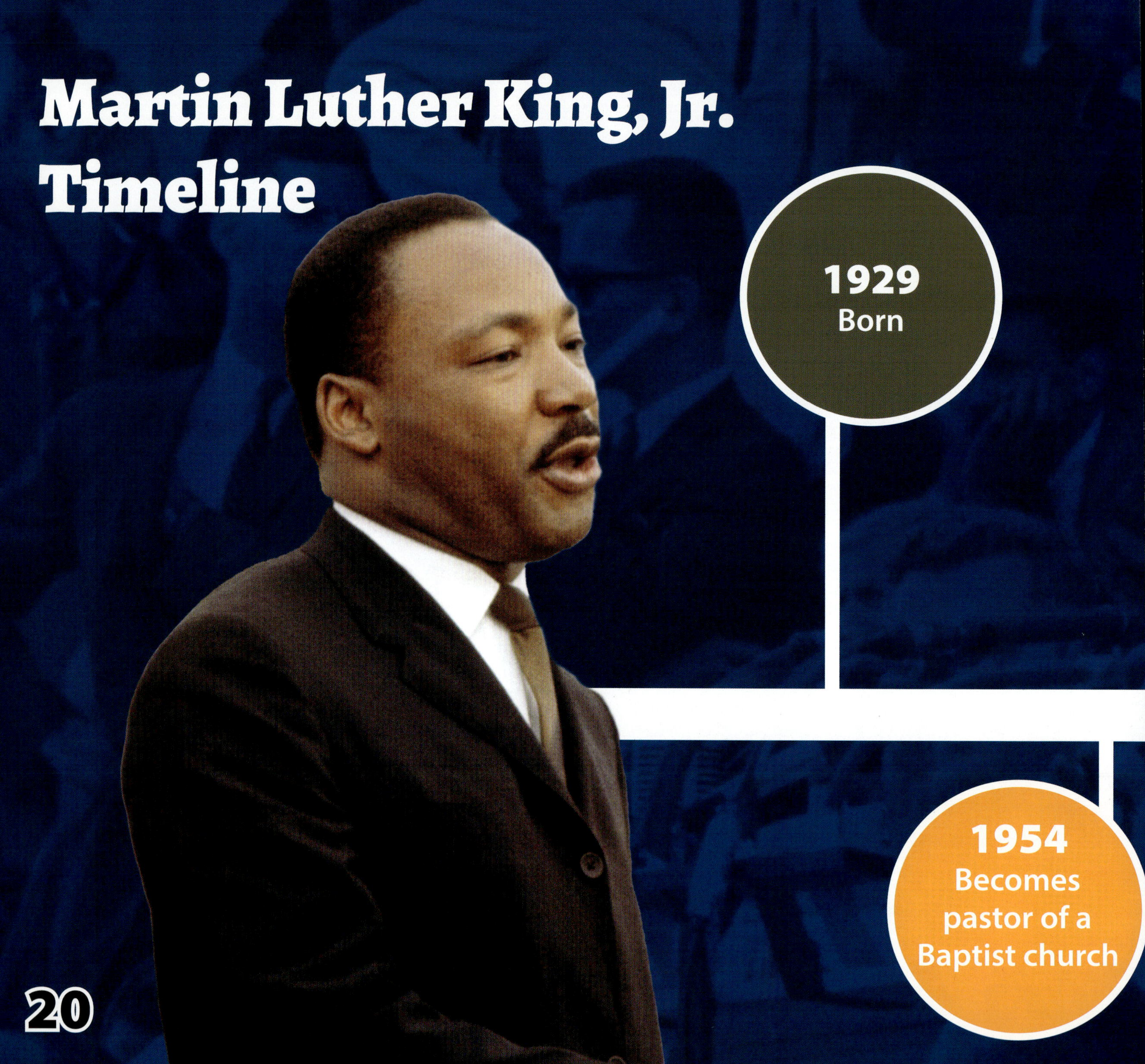

1963
Leads a march for African American rights
1964
Wins the Nobel Peace Prize
1986
Martin Luther King, Jr. Day is created
2020
55th anniversary of Selma to Montgomery March takes place
1968
Dies
2011
Martin Luther King, Jr. Memorial opens in Washington, D.C.

Cause

A cause is the reason something happens.

King was a civil rights leader.

King said African Americans should have equal rights.

Effect

An effect is the outcome.

King gave powerful speeches and led peaceful protests.

Civil rights laws were changed.

KEY WORDS

Research has shown that as much as 65 percent of all written material published in English is made up of 300 words. These 300 words cannot be taught using pictures or learned by sounding them out. They must be recognized by sight. This book contains 59 common sight words to help young readers improve their reading fluency and comprehension. This book also teaches young readers several important content words, such as proper nouns. These words are paired with pictures to aid in learning and improve understanding.

Page	Sight Words First Appearance
4	a, important, in, most, of, one, people, rights, the, to, was
6	after, are, he, his, house, more, than
8	Americans, and, did, like, not, other, some, sometimes, were
10	all, be, should, that
12	by, change, have, many, place, there
14	always, because, do, is, just, their, time, what
16	about, for
18	I, it, work
19	every, three, year
21	day, opens, takes
22	said, something
23	an

Page	Content Words First Appearance
4	civil rights, equality, history, leaders, march, Martin Luther King, Jr.
6	Georgia, grandparents, streets
8	African Americans
10	Baptist minister
12	government
14	skin
16	fairness, speeches
18	famous, "I Have a Dream," Nobel Peace Prize, today
19	Martin Luther King, Jr. Memorial, Washington, D.C.
20	church, pastor, timeline
21	anniversary, Martin Luther King, Jr. Day, Montgomery, Selma
22	cause, reason
23	effect, laws, outcome, protests, speeches

Published by Smartbook Media Inc.
350 5th Avenue, 59th Floor New York, NY 10118
Website: www.openlightbox.com

Library of Congress Cataloging-in-Publication Data

Names: Erlic, Lily, author.
Title: Martin Luther King, Jr. / Lily Erlic.
Description: New York : Smartbook Media Inc., [2021] | Series: Historical figures | "Lightbox openlightbox.com."--Title page. | Audience: Ages 4-8 | Audience: Grades K-1
Identifiers: LCCN 2020014159 (print) | LCCN 2020014160 (ebook) | ISBN 9781510553699 (library binding) | ISBN 9781510553705 | ISBN 9781510553712
Subjects: LCSH: King, Martin Luther, Jr., 1929-1968--Juvenile literature. | African Americans--Biography--Juvenile literature. | Baptists--United States--Clergy--Biography--Juvenile literature. | African Americans--Civil rights--Juvenile literature. | Civil rights workers--United States--Biography--Juvenile literature. | Civil rights movements--United States--History--20th century--Juvenile literature.
Classification: LCC E185.97.K5 E75 2021 (print) | LCC E185.97.K5 (ebook) | DDC 323.092 [B]--dc23
LC record available at https://lccn.loc.gov/2020014159
LC ebook record available at https://lccn.loc.gov/2020014160

Printed in Guangzhou, China
1 2 3 4 5 6 7 8 9 0 24 23 22 21 20

042020
110819

Project Coordinator: Priyanka Das
Designer: Ana María Vidal

Every reasonable effort has been made to trace ownership and to obtain permission to reprint copyright material. The publisher would be pleased to have any errors or omissions brought to its attention so that they may be corrected in subsequent printings.

The publisher acknowledges Alamy, Getty Images, and iStock as the primary image suppliers for this title.